I0449363

STUDENTS' COMPANION

IN

THESIS
PROPOSAL
WRITING

NORMAN A.
ABDURAHMAN, ED.D
ABUBAKAR J.
RADJUNI, MAED

Students' Companion in Thesis Proposal Writing

Copyright @ 2021 by

Norman A. Abdurahman, Ed.D.

Abubakar J. Radjuni, MAEd.

Published by

Lulu Books Publishing

United States of America

ISBN 978-1-312-31079-7

ACKNOWLEDGEMENTS

We wish to convey our thanks and profound gratitude to the following persons:

Special mention to Dr. Nagder J. Abdurahman, Chancellor of Mindanao State University - Sulu;you're your continuing support and encoragement in writing their book;

JD Abuzamier A. Asanji, the Vice Chancellor for Administration and Finance, for your support and encouragement during the drafting of this book;

Dr. McWinner Yawman, our professional Editor, for the untiring services in the proofreading and editing of the manuscript;

Our families, friends, students and collegues, for the inspirations.

And above all, to ALMIGHTY ALLAH (SWT) for the relentless blessings and guidance...

DEDICATION

We dedicated this book to our families, friends, brothers and sisters, students and collegues; especially to Chancellor, Dr. Nagder J. Abdurahman; Vice Chancellor for Administration and Finance, Jurist Doctor Abuzamier A. Asanji.

TABLE OF CONTENTS

CHAPTER 1

Format and Identifying Research Problems

Research Proposal Format

The proposal can follow the outline used for the first three chapters of the completed thesis. This format is appropriate for studies using quantitative or qualitative methodologies.[1]

There are three parts of the thesis proposal (1) The Problem: Rationale and Background (2) Related Literature Review, and (3) Research Methodology

1. The Problem: Rationale and Background (Introduction)

- Statement of the Problem
- Objectives of the Study of the Study
- Research Hypotheses
- Theoretical Framework/ Conceptual Framework
- Significance of the Study of the Study

- Scope and Limitations of the Study
- Definition of Terms

2. **Review of Related Literature**

This part consists of (1) Related legal Basis., (2) Related Literature (3) Related Studies (Local or Foreign) (4) justification of the Proposed Study, and (5) Synthesis

3. Research Methodology

- Research Design
- Research Locale
- Research Population and Samples (Sampling Procedure)
- Research Instrument (Validation of Instrument If Necessary)
- Data Gathering Procedure
- Statistical Analysis

How do you identify your research problem?

There are several factors to consider to identify.

1. Existing problems in society or the family.

2. Situation in the school.

3. Problem in the community.

4. Problem of government.

5. Problem in the workplace.

6. Problem in your relationship with your friends, classmate, and teachers alike.

Below are some Examples:

Areas	Problems
Society	Unemployment
School	Students Absenteeism
Community	Garbage Disposal
Government	Graft and Corruption
Workplace	Tardiness
Teacher's Problems	Motivation

Based on the above problems, you can now identify which topic is researchable. And that you can start to formulate your title, as shown below:

Research Title:

1. Factors That Causes Unemployment among College Graduates in Sulu.

2. Variables Related to Absenteeism Among Third Year College Of Education Students of Mindanao State University -Sulu.

3. Management of Garbage Disposal in Barangay Latih, Patikul, Sulu.

4. Graft and Corruption: Its Impact on Economic Development in the Rural Areas

5. Effect of Tardiness on the Academic Performance of Third Year College of Education Students of Mindanao State University-Sulu

6. Relationship of Teachers' Profile to Job Motivation of the Senior High School Teachers of Mindanao State University-Sulu.

You now have the hints on how to formulate a research title based on your identified problems. So, you can now start developing your Statement of the Problem (SOP) or specific issues based on the title or issue that you have.

See the Example below:

A. *Factors That Causes Unemployment among College Graduates in Sulu.*

The study aims to examine the relevant factors that cause unemployment

among college graduates in Sulu. Specifically, this study sought the answer to the following specific problems:

1. What are the factors that cause unemployment among college graduates in Sulu?

2. What are the interventions of the Tertiary institutions in Sulu to address the aggravating problems of unemployment?

3. Are there Local Government Programs of Sulu local officials to address the unemployment problems in the province?[2]

B. Variables Related to Absenteeism of Third Year College of Education Students of Mindanao State University -Sulu.

Generally, the purpose of the study is to find out the variables related to absenteeism among College of Education Students at Mindanao State University-Sulu and its effect on their academic performance. Specifically, this paper aims to answer the following questions:

1. What are the variables related to absenteeism of third-year College of Education students in Mindanao State University-Sulu.

2. What is the performance of the third-year college of education students in Mindanao State University-Sulu?

3. Is there a significant difference in the Third Year College of education Students' academic performance when grouped according to gender and marital status?

4. Is there any relationship of absenteeism with the academic performance of the third-year college of Education students?[3,4,5]

5

Activity 1:

NAME_____

Date of Submission: _____

1. Enumerate at least three (3) possible problems you may encounter in the different settings below:

1. Personal (Family and Social)

a._____

_____

b._____

_____

c._____

_____

2. School

a._____

_____

b._____

_____

C._____

_____

3. Community

a._____

_____

b._____

_____

c._____

_____

4. Workplace

a._____

_____

b._____

_____

c._____

_____

5. Government

a._____

_____

b._____

_____

c._____

_____

2. Based on the possible problems, identify at least three (3) researchable problems and explain why you chose them.

a._____

_____

_____

_____

_____

_____

_____

_____.

b._____

_____

_____

_____

_____

_____

_____

_____.

c._____

_____

_____

_____

_____

_____

_____

_____.

3. Formulate at least three (3) research titles on the basis of your identified researchable problems in no.2.

a._____
_____
_____
_____.

b._____
_____
_____
_____.

c._____
_____
_____
_____
.

CHAPTER 2

Writing the Research Proposal Introduction

The Problem

The first chapter of the research is entitled: "The Problem or The Problem and Its Background. Its purpose is to introduce the problem, clarify important variables and their delimitations, and their significance to the field of the study. It has the following essential elements:[1]

a. Introduction

b. Statement of the problem

c. Scope and delimitation

d. Significance of study

e. Notes in Chapter I

Note:

The researcher has to introduce the different elements of Chapter I by giving a brief description of each component for the reader to know what to expect of the chapter.[2]

Example:

This chapter presents the different essential elements: the introduction, which contains the rationale (an explanation of the reasons, the literature review and statistical foundation, the statement of the general and the specific problems, the scope and delimitations which identifies the major and sub- variables and the indicators, the significance of the study which enumerates the beneficiaries of the research and the corresponding benefits each will receive, and the definition of terms which unlock the most important words of the construct used in the study.

The introduction is very important in establishing the cognitive setting of the study, which involve: (1) Rationalizing why there is a need to research on the problem (the reasons for conducting the study), (2) clarifying the most important terminologies for the reader to understand what the research is all about easy, and (3) establishing the degree of seriousness of the problem which prompts the researcher to look for a solution.[3]

The following questions may help you in formulating your introduction:

1. What is the rationale of the problem? This is about sharing the beneficiaries the reasons the persuaded the writer to conduct the study. This is somewhat a narration of the writer's experience that led them to conduct an investigation.[4]

2. What is the setting of the study? This describes the place where the research will be conducted. The study location has a significant bearing on the variables of the study.

3. What is the Basic Literature of the Study? This part purports the researcher to define the terms or variables used in the study. This must be clear to the researcher so that he/she can make the reader understand them. This part is derived from various literature sources.

4. How serious is the problem? Why is there a need to look for a solution to a problem? In this aspect, the research is tasked to investigate the intensity or magnitude of the problem. Mostly, the researcher may look for quantitative or statistical evidence to assess the weight of the problem.[5]

5. What is the general objective of the problem or study? This is the general statement of the problem and should also be the basis for formulating the specific problem.

6. What is the Overall purpose of the problem? It refers to the significant contribution to the target beneficiaries such as colleagues, parents, and students alike.[6,7]

Introduction Example: *Perceived Impact of Absenteeism on The*

Academic Performance of Senior High School Students of Mindanao State University-Sulu

Most schools in the country today are suffering from mediocre performance in the academic playing field. Often, this mediocrity is attributed to the inability of the teachers to perform well in school and so as the pupils. In the case of the Autonomous Region in Muslim Mindanao (Now Bangsamoro Autonomous Region in Muslim Mindanao), performance in education is far worse compared to the national standard. From 2015 to the present, the ARMM suffers the last in the National Achievement Test in elementary and secondary levels. It is believed that this predicament is caused by so many factors- one of which is student absenteeism.[8]

In the school context, absenteeism has habitual or intentional failure from going to school (Merriam dictionary). It cannot be denied that students may miss some school activities and lessons now and then, and it may pose a problem if the student is away from school for many days. Absenteeism reduces their opportunity to grow and succeed because students miss their education time. This also results in the loss of other students' time since teachers must use the additional time to compensate, which leads to lost teaching time for all students. Students do not attend school or class for several reasons, like students are undisciplined. Therefore, it leads to problems in student education and discipline habits in future work life (Devadoss & Foltz, 2001). Absenteeism for senior high school students is considered a predictor of academic failure and leads to many other risk factors.[9]

One factor of senior high school student absenteeism is the parental factor. Parental factors are those issues that affect student absenteeism that is within the control of the parents. Also, society holds the parents responsible for providing sufficient finances, discipline, and education for their children. According to the United Nations, Declaration of the Rights of the Child (1959), the child's best interests shall be the guiding principle of those responsible for his education and guidance; that responsibility lies in the first place with his parents. Parents who lack financial resources cannot provide for their children's basic educational needs and affect student learning performance.[10]

Student attitude is also a factor of absenteeism. For example, absenteeism is the decision of the child to stay out of school without parental knowledge or consent. Illness is also a student factor since it is mainly the student who complains of being sick. Several students admitted to malingering, they are sent to school by their parents or guardians, but they do not attend, they bypass on their way to school. This will affect the student's learning performance.

Therefore, this study is designed to ascertain the effect of absenteeism on the academic performance of senior high school students in Mindanao State University – Sulu S.Y. 2018-2019 as perceived by teachers and students themselves. The researcher believes that this investigation will help the administrators and teachers come up with policy measures to reduce the cases of student absenteeism in the school, thereby leading to improved academic performance.

Activity 2

Writing the Introduction

Proposed Study (Research Title)

_____

_____

_____

1. What is the rationale of your problem/ study (Reasons for conducting the study)

_____

_____

_____

_____

_____

_____

_____

_____

_____

_____

_____

_____

_____

_____

_____

_____.

2. Describe the setting where your study is to be conducted.

_____

_____

_____

_____

_____

_____

_____

_____

_____

_____

_____

_____

_____

_____

_____

_____.

3. Look for related literature or studies that define the main concepts of your research (Collect at least three references per concept).

_____

_____

_____

_____

_____

_____

_____

_____

_____

_____

_____

_____

_____

_____

4. Determine how serious your chosen problem/study is. Show statistical evidence of its gravity. State your references.

_____

_____

_____

_____

_____

_____

_____

_____

_____

_____

_____

_____

5. What is the general objective or overall purpose of the study?

_____

_____

_____

_____

_____

_____

_____

_____

_____

_____

_____

_____

_____

_____

_____

_____

6. Who are beneficiaries of the research, and what benefits will they receive from it?

How To Write Your Statement of the Problem

After you have clarified the rationale, identified the degree of seriousness of the problem, the literature review, and the overall objective, the formulation of the heart of the thesis, the statement of the general, and the specific problems must be made.

The opening paragraph of this part of the research paper contains the general problem of the thesis. The following are examples of a widespread problem:

1. This Investigation aims to assess the perceived effect of absenteeism on the academic performance of senior high school students of Mindanao State University-Sulu SY 2020-2021.

2. The overall purpose of this study is to assess the intrapersonal and interpersonal competencies of school managers and how they contribute to school effectiveness in the schools' division of Sulu 2021.

3. The study focuses on how students, teachers, and school-related factors affect the performance of the senior high school students of Mindanao State University-Sulu Sy 2020-2021.[11]

After which, the general problem is followed by an enumeration of a specific problem. The particular problems are usually stated as questions the researcher seeks to answer.

Example:

Statement of the Problem

This investigation aims to assess the perceived effect of absenteeism on the academic performance of senior high school students of Mindanao State University-Sulu SY 2020-2021. Specifically, this research is guided by the following queries:[12]

1.   What is the perception of the teachers on the effect of absenteeism on the academic performance of senior high school students in Mindanao State University-Sulu?

2. What is the students' perception of the effect of absenteeism on the academic performance of senior high school students in Mindanao State University-Sulu?

3. Is there any significant difference in the effect of absenteeism on the academic performance of senior high school students in Mindanao State University-Sulu as perceived by the teachers and the students?

Note: The opening paragraph above is the general problem of the research paper, followed by the three specific questions.

Activity 3

Statement of the Problem

Directions: Formulate "the statement of the problem" part of your research.

Title of your research

:_____

_____

_____

_____

_____

_____

_____.

General Problem:

The researcher aims to

_____

_____

_____

_____

_____

_____

_____

_____

_____

_____

_____
_____
_____
_____._

Specific Problems:

Specifically, This study seeks to answer the following questions:

1._____
_____
_____
_____
_____.

2._____
_____
_____
_____
_____.

3._____
_____
_____
_____

How To Write Your Scope and Delimitation and Significance of the Study

How to Write Your Scope and Delimitation

This section discusses:

1.   Specific areas of investigation

2.   The Research Problem and Method

3.   Location, time and resources, the instrument, the limitation, and the delimitation of the study

The scope is the coverage of the study. The delimitation is the freedom of the researcher which topic and variables to focus on, and the limitation speaks about the incapacity, built-in weaknesses, and constraints during the conduct of the study.

Sample Scope and Delimitation:

Title: Interpersonal and Supervisory Skills of the school Administrators of Luuk National High School

Scope and Delimitation

This study will focus on the school administrator's interpersonal and supervisory skills and their impact on the school organizational climate of Luuk National High School S.Y 2020-2021. The school administrators include the school principal, head teachers, and all department heads of the said school. The administrator's Intrapersonal and technical skills are not included in the study. School climates will only cover two dimensions- teachers' dimension and administrators' dimensions. Considering the Covid-19 crisis today, accessibility to the respondents is projected to be the limitation of the study.

A questionnaire to be validated by the panel members or experts will be the main instrument of the study. A follow-up interview will also be done to clarify vague answers. This study will use mean to assess the level of interpersonal and supervisory skills of the school administrators. It will use a T-test to determine the relationship between interpersonal and supervisory skills and determine the impact of interpersonal and supervisory skills on school organizational climate.

Activity4

write your own scope and delimitation on the basis of the title of your research:

Research Title :

_____

_____

_____

_____

_____.

Scope and delimitation:

_____

_____

_____

_____

_____

_____

_____

_____

_____

_____

_____

_____

_____

How to write the significance of the study

• You have to start writing your significance of the study with a short introductory paragraph. These are few sentences that introduce the direct beneficiaries of your research.

• Of course, you have to identify your direct beneficiaries.

• Then, you have to explain the specific benefits to the specific beneficiary. Ex. School Division superintendent, principal, teachers, parents, and students, and the like. This will also include line organizations like MSU-Sulu, IPHO, MBHTE, etc.,

Finally, arrange them based on the degree of significance.[13]

Sample Significance of the study

Title: Interpersonal and Supervisory Skills of the school Administrators of Luuk National High School

Significance of the Study

This study is important for it brings out the leadership and supervisory skills of the school administrators and the description of Luuk National High School's organizational climate and the relationship that exists among them. Further, it bears significance to the number of people involved in the educational process.

For the School Administrators, the study's findings may provide different insights on how school administrators can easily relate to their teachers to improve the entire school organizational climate.

The information derived from this research could provide the respondents- school administrators of Luuk National High School- insights on enhancing their interpersonal or human relations and supervisory skills. The researcher could provide a database of information for future reference. Likewise, the findings could showcase ideas and suggestions for improving their management skills, specifically in dealing with subordinates and establishing a good rapport and stable relationships.

This would serve as a tool for school administrators for self-analysis and reflection. Moreover, this investigation will guide the principal, head teachers, and department heads to be more effective in the workplace. It will help identify and clarify the problems and issues related to human relations and supervisory activities. This may encourage the entire educational community to extend more cooperation and supports for a healthy school climate.

For the Schools Division Superintendent and the Supervisory Staff, the information derived from the study can be used as a springboard for future action plans that would further the development of educational leadership towards efficiency, effectiveness, and productivity.[14]

For Future Administrators, this investigation will also provide insights into developing their interpersonal and supervisory skills. It would also prepare them in advance on how to upgrade such skills to be ready for the challenges and complexities of administrative responsibilities that lie ahead of them.

School organizations and other officials would be provided with information on the necessity of improving the school climate to respond to the changing demands brought about by internal and external pressures in the educational landscape.

For Other Researchers, the results will be used for their possible literature for their studies. Enrichment or validation of the study is highly recommended for them to be able to reinforce the results of the investigation. This study will be a source of another research problem and can be replicated using additional variables in another locale or setting and with different respondents.

Activity 5

Write the significance of your study based on the title of your research:

Research Title :

_____

_____

_____

_____

_____.

Significance of the study:

_____

_____

_____

_____

_____

_____

_____

_____

_____

_____

_____

_____

_____

_____

_____

Conceptual framework.

It is a presentation of the relationship of various variables, concepts, or methods used in the research. It is a combination of visual and textual presentation. David (2002) taught that C.F. explains in detail the variables to be used or observed in the research and presents the assumed connection, relation, or association between and among independent and dependent variables (Amorado, Boholano, & Talili, 2017).

It also presents the researcher's way of understanding and concepts based on previous readings and experiences relative to the field or focus of the investigation. It elaborates the research problem concerning relevant literature.

It should deal with the matter such as:

1. Existing literature and previous research and its relevance to the current investigation.

2. Key ideas/concepts/construct in the research approach.

3. Possible lines/consideration of inquiry to be tracked.

4.   Relevant theoretical/conceptual perspective/s based on the previous research studies conducted and literature review.

Comparison of Theoretical and Conceptual Framework

Theoretical Framework	Conceptual Framework
Based on theories formulated by other experts	Based on concepts perceived by experts and researchers.
Require understanding of the theory	Require creativity and expertise of the researcher/s
Must be quoted	Need not be quoted
Based on propositions/systems which were previously tested and can still be tested	Generalizations are based on facts that have a widespread application based on a causal relationship between acts and their perceived consequences.
Expressed formally	They are usually expressed informally.

Similarities of Both Frameworks

1. They lead the formulation of hypothesis/es.

2. They serve as the basis for the evaluation of a theory.

3. They justify the research study.

4. They provide a system for achieving creative evaluation of the problem.

5. They direct the research.

How To write Theoretical framework and Conceptual framework and definition of Terms

How to Write Theoretical Framework?

1. You begin with identifying existing theories which link to the study.

2. Then identify key concepts in your study to comprehend the role of the theory in your study.

3. Be reminded that theories are useful devices for interpreting, criticizing, and unifying specific laws or facts that guide in discovering new generalizations (Calmorin, 2016).

Sample Theoretical Framework of the Study

This study is anchored on Carl Jung's Theory of Personality to relate the importance of understanding the factors that motivate people so school administrators can internalize how to deal with individual personalities in the school setting.. Roberds - Baxter (1986) relates Carl Jung's theory of personality to school administration, which is based upon the premise that human behavior can be categorized by type. The author accomplishes this by demonstrating how principals can utilize Jung's behavior theory to predict how individuals will perform various tasks, ultimately getting people of diverse personalities motivated to work towards common goals.[15]

Essentially Jung's theory consists of three modes: perceiving functions, judging functions, and orientation to the environment. People are born with tendencies towards preferring one mode over the others. As people grow, they become more proficient in their preferred mode, forming clusters identified as personality types. When school administrators can identify personality types, they can differentiate between people and use each individual's talents to increase team cooperation and efficiency.[15]

How to write the Conceptual Framework

1. You have to present well-defined concepts or variables in the study.

2. Then, you have to make a model or paradigm showing the relationship of the variables in the study.

3.   Finally, you have to briefly explain your model or paradigm according to the boxes and arrows pointing to the relationship of your variables.

Sample Conceptual Framework of the Study

Figure 1.1 shows the relationship between Interpersonal and Supervisory skills of the school administrators and their possible impact on school organizational climates.

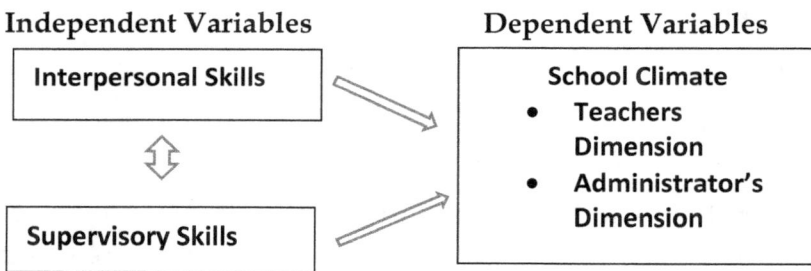

FIGURE 1.1 : Relationship of Administrators' Interpersonal and supervisory skills and their impact on school climate

This conceptual paradigm reflects how the variables interplay in the investigations. The two boxes on the left side are the independent variables of administrators' interpersonal and supervisory skills. They are interlinking with the double-headed arrows, which predict the possible relationship between the variables. Further, the box on the right side, which contains the School climate, is the dependent variable. The arrows pointing from the independent variables to the dependent variable predict the possible impact of the former on the latter.

How to Write the Definition of Terms

You have to consider the following:

1.   Identify significant concepts, terms, and variables, whether in the Title, SOP, hypothesis, paradigm, or any part of the paper.

2.   Some of them may refer to respondents, variables or sub-variables

3.   Terms that are defined must be arranged alphabetically

4.   Come up with an opening statement or paragraph before the list of terms being defined.

5.   The researcher is advised to use two ways (Conceptual definition and operational definition).

6.   But most experts highly recommend using the operational definition instead of the Conceptual definition

Sample Definition of Terms

Topic: Interpersonal and Supervisory Skills of School Administrators: Their Impact on School Climate

For purposes of clarity and greater understanding of the study, the following terms are hereby defined operationally.

Interpersonal Skills. As used in the study, this refers to the ability of the school administrators to relate effectively with subordinates, superiors, and representatives from other school organizations, Local Government Units, and other similar organizations.

Supervisory Skills. As used in the study, this term refers to the ability of the administrators to examine and engage in teacher's daily activities to improve individual and school performance. This involves monitoring, communicating, classroom visits, and the like.

School Climate. This term refers to the total environment quality within a school (Lunnenberg and Ornstein, 1991). this study relates to the present condition of Luuk National High school in terms of the human relationship among teachers themselves and between teachers and the school administrators. This entails the teachers' dimension and school administrators' dimensions.

Luuk NHS. This term refers to the school organization belonging to the Ministry of Basic, Higher and Technical education, BARMM. It is chosen to be the locale of the study for convenience and accessibility. It comprises more than 30 faculty members for junior and senior high schools headed by the school principal.

School Administrators. In this study, this term refers to the school principal, academic heads, and senior high school department coordinator. This doesn't include the master teachers who do not have an administrative position.[16]

Activity 6

Directions: Write your own theoretical and conceptual framework based on the title of your study.

Title:_____

_____

_____

_____

Theoretical Framework :

_____

_____

_____

_____

_____

_____

_____

_____

_____

_____

_____

_____

Conceptual Framework:

_____

_____

_____

_____

_____

_____

_____

_____

Definition of terms: (Give at least three words/ terms)

1._____

_____

_____

_____

2._____

_____

_____

_____

_____.

3._____

_____

_____

_____

_____

_____.

Chapter 3

Writing the Research Proposal
Review of Related Literature

What is a Review of Related Literature?

Review of Related literature covers practically all the data or information which are authoritative, relevant, and pertinent to the subject of the study. It includes all related research literature, studies, and research, including published or unpublished academic and scientific papers. The Review of Related Literature and studies could serve as the foundation of the study and tentative answer or solution to the problems. The following are the basic contents of the chapter on the review of literature.[1]

A.   Related literature- these are published articles, books, journals, magazines, novels, poetry, and other materials that directly bear the study.

B.   Related studies-these are published or unpublished studies which have a direct bearing on the study. (they are segregated into foreign and local (if any).

C.   Legal basis – laws, constitution, department orders, and memoranda have direct bearings on the study.

D.   Synthesis of all the literature and studies /Justification of the Proposed Study- these are the justification of the researchers, the direct bearings of the literature, related studies, and related legal basis to the study. Also, the researcher will justify the difference of the related studies with the previous studies.

Purpose of Literature Review

> To indicate the research that has been conducted in the area before, to ensure that you're not 'reinventing the wheel.'

> To demonstrate that you're aware of the important and recent studies in your study area

> To ensure that you haven't missed literature detailing a novel way for you to conduct your study

> To explain the theoretical background to the proposed research project

> To demonstrate your ability to analyze the literature in your study area critically.

> To identify gap to justify the contribution of your research project is to the growing body of literature

> To learn more about your chosen methodology, specifically on the authors' philosophy that suggest them.

Importance of Literature Review

A.   It is a realization that at the start of any worthwhile project, an idea has already been thought of before, at least to some degree.

B.   "...Libero   (2008)   emphasizes   that   a comprehensive review of the literature would greatly help the thesis student in determining the research gaps in the area of his/her study, as well as in providing a synthesis of the latest development in the discipline..."

C.   MacMillan (2016) says that a literature review refines the research problem, establishes the conceptual or theoretical framework, helps develop the significance of the study, research questions, and hypotheses, assists in identifying the strengths and limitations of the research methodology, enables the researchers to identify contradictory findings.[2]

D.   "...it documents how your study adds to existing literature.

Sources of Literature Review

1. Primary
2. Secondary

Types of Literature Review

1. Conceptual Literature
2. Research Literature

The Literature Review Process

a. Select a Topic

b. Select and choose literature

c. Analyze and interpret literature

d. Write the review

Structure of Literature Review

1. By author
2. By topic
3. Chronological

4. From general concepts to specific concepts or vice- versa
5. By theme
6. By Type of Research

How to Write Review of Related Literature?

1. Write a short introductory paragraph

2. Present your literature systematically according to the importance

3. It is recommended to make sub-heading according to variables starting with major variables and sub-variables in the study or according to categories such as related literature, related studies, and related legal bases.

4. End your RRL with at least one paragraph for the justification of your study or synthesis of your study

Sample Review of Related Literatures

Title: *Interpersonal and Supervisory of the School Administrators of Luuk National High School*

This chapter presents some related literature and studies which contain the major and minor variables in the study. This includes the interpersonal and supervisory skills of the school administrators and the school organizational climate, which entail the teachers' and administrators' dimensions. This literature serves as the foundation that gives some direct bearings to the problems of the study.

Related Literature on Interpersonal Skills

Developing effective interpersonal skills and implementing them in a school setting does not mean that administrators are not responsible for insisting on a high level of staff performance. Administrators are responsible for taking appropriate action when an individual's performance does not meet the district's expectations or the administrator's.[3]

In these cases, an administrator must be more than someone sensitive to people's needs—he must also be a leader, willing to take risks and make decisions which he feels will benefit the overall good of the school. Being trained to recognize and understand human behavior does not make it easier to make these decisions. However, human relations training will add to the skill administrators need in predicting outcomes, choosing among alternatives, and helps in the problem-solving process (Savage, 1968).[3]

Administrators must realize that even though disagreement may occur, it is still possible to work with people. It would be very unusual for everyone on staff to agree on every matter with the administrator; if they did, little diversity or creativity would occur, resulting in fostering mediocrity and conformity. An agreement, of course, must exist within a staff on basic principles, but seeking full unanimity results in ineffective administration that prevents progress (Savage, 1968). As important as interpersonal relation skills are to an administrator.

Giammatteo and Giammatteo (1981) discussed interpersonal skills in the context of leadership. They explained that leaders best know how to motivate and involve those with whom they work. The skills associated with effective leadership are all related to interpersonal relations skills. The skills of leadership include; 1) Skills of personal behavior-- where the leader is sensitive to the needs of the group, listens attentively and refrains from ridiculing or criticizing members' suggestions; 2) skills of communication -- the leader effectively communicates why things are done as a matter of routine; 3) skills of equality -- the leader recognizes that everyone is important and shares leadership because he recognizes that leadership cannot be monopolized; 4) skills of self-examination --the leader is aware of the motives and action-guiding his behavior and counters hostilities by being tolerant of member's views helping them become aware of their own forces, attitudes, and values. These interpersonal skills are eminently learnable and can be honed through practice, diligence, and study.[3]

Related Literature on Supervisory Skills

A supervisor's words and actions greatly impact the behavior of subordinates and the organization's responsiveness to leadership efforts. Consider the case of a second lieutenant given a task by his commander to improve the performance of his associates. A few months later, the subordinates had already forgotten everything the lieutenant had discussed with them during their first meeting. Except for his opening statement, they would never forget that: "I have been sent in to straighten things out around here." At that moment, resistance to his leadership was born. If asked, many of the subordinates could probably have suggested changes to improve the organization. However, the lieutenant didn't ask. He told them, and they resisted every change he sought to introduce.[4]

Supervision isn't an armchair occupation, nor does "getting involved" means running your section "by decree" from a closed office. It means getting out and understanding the day-to-day operation firsthand. It means knowing your people as individuals and being known by them. Real involvement on the part of the supervisor reaps two advantages. First, it will provide you with knowledge about your section that is unobtainable any other way. Secondly, frequent interaction with your people promotes what managerial experts call a "therapeutic climate"--the supervisor demonstrates concern for the workers' daily performance, rather than taking it for granted. Visible and personal involvement by the supervisor builds morale and a sense of cohesion within the entire section. This forms a substantial base for a productive supervisor-subordinate relationship.[4]

Related Studies

A study by Terry A. Thomas (1971) demonstrated that a significant relationship existed between human relations training and a principal's effectiveness. The study indicated that principals who were trained in human relations became more aware of the individual needs of staff members and dealt with staff more tactfully, resulting in a higher degree of staff morale. Principals who were trained in human relations techniques viewed teachers who assumed responsibility to be an asset to their schools rather than a threat to their authority and consequently used democratic decision-making strategies rather than autocratic strategies in dealing with problems. The study also indicated that when principals utilize human relations techniques in teacher supervision, teacher performance improved. Savage (1968, p.7) elaborates: The school administrator must understand his behavior and the behavior of pupils, teachers, other staff members, parents, and all community citizens who influence educational policy in any way.[4]

He must understand the group dynamics of school boards, school-related organizations such as the parent teacher association, and groups of school personnel, and the many other groups in the community that can or do affect the operation, strength, and qualities of schools. Unlike the executive in business or industry, the school administrator is responsible to a superior and/or controlling school board and the community in general. Therefore, his perspective of interpersonal and group behavior must be broader. The retention of his position is dependent; in this perspective, the quality of education provided for the children enrolled in the school or schools for which he is responsible depends on his knowledge and skills in human relations.[4]

The key element underlying effective school administration is an administrator's ability to communicate with, understand, and influence the people he comes in contact with. Proficiency in interpersonal skills affects the implementation of the entire spectrum of administrative tasks. To influence change and promote a climate of cooperation and growth, an administrator must be capable of recognizing, internalizing, and applying these skills. This paper, then, focuses attention on the importance of interpersonal relations skills in school administration.[4]

Note: The search for a legal basis for this particular topic is still in progress.

Activity 6

Directions: Write your review of related literature based on the title of your study.

Title:_____

_____

_____

_____

Introductory paragraph

_____

_____

_____

_____

_____

_____

_____

Related Literatures :

_____

_____

_____

_____

_____

Related Studies :

_____

_____

Synthesis/justification:_____

_____

_____

_____

_____

_____

_____

_____

_____

_____

_____.

Chapter 4

Writing the Research Proposal Methodology

The methodology is used as the middle heading of descriptive design. This is presented in Chapter 3 of a thesis or dissertation. It consists of the following parts such as (1) Research design, (2) Research Locale (3) Sampling design, (4) Subjects or respondents of the study (5) The research instrument (6) Data Gathering procedure (7) Statistical treatment

Research Design

The student uses this section to describe the research design chosen to frame the study (e.g. case study, experimental design, narrative, survey design, action research, single-subject) and to justify this design by linking characteristics of the design, as found in the research methods literature, to aims and objectives of the student's investigation. This section also outlines and describes the chosen methodology or approach (e.g., positivist, interpretivist, critical theory) underpinning the design and the methods (e.g., qualitative, quantitative, conceptual, philosophical) by which data will be collected and analyzed.[1]

Research Locale

The researchers have to identify the exact location of the study. If possible, they also have to explain the reasons for choosing the location. They have to include description of the organizational structure and the number of personnel working there.

Sampling Design

There are two kinds of sampling designs. These are (1) scientific sampling or probability sampling and (2) non-scientific or non-probability sampling. The former is preferable because every member of the society is given an equal chance to being included in the sample.

When relevant, this must be identified for all research designs. Students should specify the type of sampling that is expected to be employed and describe the steps taken to gain access and solicit participation. Sampling options include:

1. Simple random sampling
2. Stratified random sampling
3. Cluster sampling

4. Systematic sampling
5. Convenience sampling
6. Purposive sampling
7. Snowball sampling
8. Reputational sampling

Research Respondents

The researchers have to explain how and where the subject will be taken from. If possible, they have to explain why they selected them to be the respondents of the study. They can either take all of the population if it is less than 100. But if the population is too large, 100 or more, they can simply take a portion of it.

Research Instrument

This section specifies the instrument that should be used to collect data and the procedures that will be followed. Research instruments can be borrowed from others or developed by the researcher. If students create their questionnaire for quantitative studies, it should be pilot tested and checked for content and face validity. If instruments are borrowed, written permission must be sought for use. If possible, students should only use instruments that are valid and reliable. Statements about validity and reliability must be included in the proposal.[1]

For qualitative studies, students must outline the questions they expect to ask in an interview or the types of items they will look for in an observation. Thesis must be accompanied by an explanation of how the student decided on these questions/ items (e.g., from specific concepts in the literature, from a previous study, or from some other source). If the student plans to analyze documents, the proposal must specify which documents will be collected, where they can be found, and how they advance the investigation.[2]

Data Gathering Procedure

After validating the research instrument, the researchers have to outline how they can gather data. Here, the researchers have to start with asking permission from the agency's head where the respondents are employed. Once permitted, the researchers have to proceed with the launching of the questionnaire to the respondents. They also state the date of the retrieval and the percentage retrieval of the instrument. For example, there are 100 questionnaires administered to the 100 respondents of the study, but only 98 were retrieved. Hence, this must be stated that out of 100 questionnaires launched to the study respondents, only 98 or 98% were retrieved.

Data Analysis

The proposal must indicate how the student plans to analyze the data to generate answers to the research question. It is helpful to think about analysis in relation to the empirical questions listed in the Purpose section. Students should consider which data elements are likely to address each of the empirical questions and what they might do with the data to derive an answer. Quantitative analyses should be attached to research hypotheses and can include descriptive, parametric, and nonparametric statistics. The type of test used should be specified for each hypothesis, and students might also provide a preliminary version of the form within which the findings will be displayed: chart, graph, and/ or table. It is essential that quantitative terminology and statistical tests are clearly understood and appropriately used in the research proposal. Therefore, students planning on using quantitative methodology are well advised to take a statistics course (e.g., EDUC 8100).[1]

Qualitative analyses can be approached from a within-case and/ or cross-case perspective using an inductive and/ or deductive approach. The type of analysis should be matched to the purpose of the study and specific study questions. Students should also give some consideration to how the data will be organized and displayed. It is essential that qualitative terminology and analytic tools are clearly understood and appropriately used in the research proposal. Therefore, students planning on using qualitative methodology are well-advised to take a qualitative research course (e.g., EDUC 8300).[3]

Sample Methodology

Chapter III

METHODOLOGY

This chapter presents the processes or methods to be used in the study. This includes the research design, research locale, respondents, research instrument, validation of the research instrument, data gathering procedure, and the statistical tool used in the study.

Research Design

This is study will use descriptive-correlational research. It is descriptive because the self-made data gathering instruments will be analyzed and interpreted to describe the level of interpersonal and supervisory skills of the school administrators in Luuk National High School. This also includes the assessment of the condition of school organizational climate. This is correlational because it describes the relationship between administrators' interpersonal and supervisory skills and their impact on school organizational climate.

Gay (1976), as cited by Cristobal and Cristobal Jr. (2013), defined descriptive research as involving the current status of the subject of the study. This method of analysis is designed to gather information on conditions existing at a particular period. Similarly, A correlation approach will be used to relate the interpersonal skills of the school administrators with their supervisory skills. According to Calmorin (1998), as cited by Cristobal and Cristobal Jr (2013), a Correlational study is used to determine the relationship of variables. It tries to point out how the different variables are related to each other in the target population. It also ascertains how much variation is caused by another variable.[4,5]

Research Locale

The study setting will be at Luuk National High school, located in the eastern hemisphere of the province of Sulu. Said school belongs to the second congressional legislative district, approximately 60-kilometer from the capital town of the province-municipality of Jolo. Luuk national NHS has been continuously serving thousands of students every year, ranging from junior to senior high school department l. It is currently managed by a school principal with more than twenty faculty members from two departments. The researcher has chosen this school as the study's setting for the following reasons: first, it has greater accessibility considering that the researcher is currently connected at the said school. Second, the researcher feels that there is a need for the school administrator' to be given feedback on their performance to reflect and learn. Third, this research work will hope to provide insights to the administrators and teachers to improve the school climate.

Sampling Design

The researcher will have a total enumeration of the respondents. It means that all faculty members Luuk NH, including junior and senior high school, will be taken as participants of the study. These respondents will answer the self-made questionnaire after being validated by the panel members or experts. They will be the ones that determine the level of Interpersonal and supervisory skills manifested by the school administrators. And they will also be assessing the condition of the school climate of the said school.

Research Respondents

All the faculty members and school heads of Luuk National High School will be taken as respondents. Faculty members include senior high school and junior high school. The researcher opted to choose the subject of the study because she is currently connected to the same institution. Hence it will be easy for her to access each of them at their residence.

Research Instrument

After a thorough library works of the review of related literature and studies, the researcher will finally come up with a self-made questionnaire to be validated by the panel members or experts.

According to Padua (2001) in Cristobal Jr & Cristobal (2013), a questionnaire is a list of planned, written questions related to a particular topic with a space provided for the response to each question. In like manner, the questionnaire is commonly used in a normative survey and in measuring attitudes (Good: 1991). In other words, the questionnaire is the best instrument that can supply the necessary information to complete a research study as it is commonly used in Behavioral science research or social research (Calderon & Gonzalez: 2005).[6]

It is composed of three parts: The first part is an assessment of interpersonal skills as manifested by the school administrators at Luuk NHS. The second part entails the school administrators' supervisory skills, and the last part evaluates the school organizational climate.

Data Gathering Procedure

The researcher will seek permission from the graduate school Dean, Dr. Magna Annisa Edding Hayudini, to launch the research questionnaire. Once approved, the researcher will now send a letter to the School Division Superintendent for Dr. Kiram Irilis, asking permission to launch the investigation on the subject. Upon approval, the researcher will now send a letter to the school principal of Luuk NHS to conduct the study. The respondents will be asked to answer the questionnaire fairly about how they feel in the school organization as the interpersonal and supervisory skills of the school administrators and the school organizational climate.

Then, the questionnaire will be retrieved by the researcher a day after.[7]

Statistical Tool

To treat the empirical data, Mean will be used to analyze the interpersonal and supervisory skills of the school administrators. Similarly, the Mean will also be used to assess the organizational climate of Luuk National High School. Moreover, Correlation will be used to find out the relationship of interpersonal and supervisory skills of the school administrators to organizational climate.

Activity 7

A.   Write your Chapter 3 (Methodology) based on the title of the study.

Research Design

_____

_____

_____

_____

_____

_____

_____

_____

_____

_____

_____

Research Locale

_____

_____

_____

_____

_____

_____

_____

_____

_____

_____

_____

_____

_____

_____

_____

_____

_____.

Sampling Design/ Technique

_____

_____

_____

_____

_____

_____

_____

_____

_____

_____

_____

_____

_____

_____

_____

_____

_____

_____

_____.

Research Respondents

_____

_____

_____

_____

_____

_____

_____

_____

_____

_____

_____

_____

_____.

Research Design

_____

_____

_____

_____

_____

_____

_____

_____

_____

_____

_____

_____

Research Instrument

_____

_____

_____

_____

_____

_____

_____

_____

_____

_____

_____

_____

_____

_____

_____

_____.

Data Gathering Procedure

_____

_____

_____

_____

_____

_____

Statistical Tool

CHAPTER 5

Citing Sources

a.   **The Need for Citing Sources**

There are two reasons; a) to avoid plagiarism and b) to assign proper authority to a statement.

b.   **Referencing Sources**

Referencing your sources means systematically showing what information or ideas you are quoting or paraphrasing from another author's works and where they come from. As a dictum, you must research to do research.

Referencing appropriately is important for some reasons, as stated below.

• Adds authority to your work by supporting it with previous research

• Demonstrates reading and understanding of relevant literature

• Enables the reader to track down the sources to check their quality (and to check that you haven't misinterpreted them)

• Ensures that you write ethically by giving credit to the original authors (Dempster & Hanna, 2016)

c. **Categories of Sources**

Documents. Both printed and written materials can be categorized into published and unpublished

e.g. annual reports, books, artworks, cartoons, circulars, records, diaries, notebooks

Numerical Records. Subcategory of documents and any type of numerical data in printed form.

e.g. test scores, attendance figures, census reports, school budget

Oral Statements. Any materials that leave a record for the future generations

e.g. stories, myth, tales, legends, chants, songs

Relics. Any objects can provide some information about the past.

e.g. Furniture, artwork, clothing, building, equipment

d. **Synthesis and Its Types**

Synthesis is the discussion that draws on one or more sources. It also refers to bringing together materials from different sources and the creation of an integrated whole.

The following are the two types of synthesis:

1.   Explanatory synthesis. Aim to present the facts in a reasonably objective manner.

2.   Argument synthesis. Aim to present your point of view with the support of relevant facts drawn from services and presented logically.

What is a citation?

A citation, or reference, is the quoting, paraphrasing, or summarizing of someone else's work, used as a basis for another's ideas and research. A citation also refers to the information about a source, such as a title, author, date, etc., which gives credit to the original author and shows readers where to find the original work. There are two parts to a citation: the in-text citation or parenthetical citation, which goes next to the quoted material, and the reference list citation or bibliography, found at the end of a paper or report. This list is also called a bibliography. This paper deals specifically with bibliographic citation. [1,2]

Citations should follow a standardized format from a style guide such as APA (American Psychological Association) or MLA (Modern Language Association).

When to cite

Citation is necessary to use anything that is not common knowledge, including when a word-for-word quote is not used but the main ideas or heart of a passage are still described (called paraphrasing). But citing sources is more than just avoiding plagiarism. Citations give credibility to work, and references strengthen work by putting it into meaningful context.[1]

This paper is a compilation of the recognized citation styles and is organized according to the various disciplines. One is not stipulated to use a particular style simply because it is the recognized style for a particular discipline but rather to choose the best method to suit their purpose. In the case of students, it is recommended that they check with their lecturers before choosing a citation style.[3]

Why do you need to use a citation format?

1. Allows readers to cross-reference your resources easily.
2. Provides consistent format within a discipline.
3. Gives you credibility as a writer.
4. Protects you from plagiarism

Consistency in citing of sources

One must use a consistent format when citing sources. Basic elements of a citation must include, at a minimum, author (if there is one; Title; Publication details (place of publication, publisher, date). Using a consistent format helps your reader to understand your arguments and the sources they are built on. It also allows you to keep track of your sources as you develop your arguments.[4]

The Various Citation Styles

a.   American Psychological Association (APA). Author-date-based style and commonly used in psychology and education

b.   Modern Language Association (MLA). Author-page-based style and most often applied in arts and humanities.

c.   Harvard. Style is very similar to APA, and most well used referencing style in U.K. and Australia and use in humanities.

d.   Chicago & Turabian. Two separate styles but very similar and widely used in history and economics.

Ethical Standards in Writing Related Literature

Ethical standards here may refer to the rules and standards in writing research in any profession, also known as Research Ethics. Research ethics are standardized rules that guide the design and conduct of research (Dempster and Hanna, 2016). The term "ethics" refers to questions of right and wrong.[5]

If the writer may not follow the standard rules in research, s/he may be committed a crime known as plagiarism. The word "plagiarism" was taken from the word "plagiarize" means "to steal and pass off (the ideas and words of another) as one's own without crediting the source; to commit literary theft; present as new and original an idea or product derived from existing source" (2006).[6]

Plagiarism is committed when authors present the words, data, or ideas with the implication that they are their own, without attribution. This act is against the Intellectual Property Rights Law. It is a form of research misconduct.[7]

Suppose there is a word-for-word copying beyond a short phrase or six or seven words of someone else's text. In that case, that section should be enclosed in quotation marks or indented and referenced at the location in the manuscript of the copied materials to the source.[8]

The work of others should be cited and credited, whether published and unpublished, and whether it had been written for an oral presentation or materials on the website.

Top Plagiarism Practices (White Paper on Plagiarism Spectrum by Turnitin.com)

1.   Cloning

2.   CTRL – C

3.   Mash-up

APA Styles of Citation Format for References/Bibliography

Introduction

American Psychological Association, commonly known as APA Referencing, is very similar to that of Harvard Referencing Style

Where Harvard is most commonly used in U.K. and Australia, APA is more popular in the USA. Although there is not much variation in the formatting, before using a particular guide, you need to take caution about what style your institution demands.[9]

The guide in the following section has been adopted from APA 6th edition Library guide for the University of Sydney.

APA style throughout the text requires double line spacing, worthy of mentioning it is also necessary for the reference section.

Disciplines using the style:

It is mostly used in the various fields of social sciences.

It is also used in some other areas such as business, education, and nursing.

i. Journal

Journal Article in Print:

<Name of author/s>. (<Publication Year>). <Article title>. <Journal title>, <volume number> (<Issue number>), <range of page numbers>.

Article from e-Journal:

<Name of author/s>. (<Publication Year>). <Article title>. <Journal title>, <volume number> (<Issue number>), <range of page numbers>. Retrieved from <URL>[9]

Example:

Towler, A. J., & Schneider, D. J. (2005). Distinctions among stigmatized groups. Journal of Applied Social Psychology, 35, 1-14.

Miles, L. (2000). Constructing composition: Reproduction and WPA agency in textbook publishing. Writing Program Administration, 24(1-2), 27-51.

Nespor, M., & Sandler, W. (1999). Prosody in Israeli sign language [Abstract]. Language and Speech, 42, 143.

Kensinger, E. A., Krendl, A. C., & Corkin, S. (2005). Memories of an Emotional and a nonemotional event: Effects of aging and delay interval [Electronic version]. Experimental Aging Research, 32, 23-45.

Viano, M. (1999). Life is beautiful: Reception, allegory, and holocaust laughter. Jewish Social Studies, 5(3), 47-66. Retrieved February 28, 2006, from http://muse.jhu.edu/demo/jewish_social_studies/v0 05/5.3viano.html

Moss, S. A., & Ngu, S. (2006). The relationship between personality and leadership preferences. Current Research in Social Psychology, 11(6), 70-91. Retrieved February 28, 2006, from http://www.uiowa.edu/~grpproc/Crisp/crisp11_6.p df [11,12]

McArt, E., Shulman, D., & Gajary, E. (1999). Developing an educational workshop on teen depression and suicide: A proactive community intervention. Child Welfare, 78(6), 793-806. Retrieved January 3, 2006, from PsychINFO database.

ii. Books

Book with an Author:

<Name of author>. (<Publication Year>). <Book Title> (<Edition>). <Place of Publication>: <Publisher>.

Example:

Bazerman, C. (2002). The languages of Edison's light. Cambridge, MA: MIT Press.

Book with more than one author:

• For books with more than one author, every piece of information remains the same as the book with one author

• To find how the authors' names are written, follow the section "What to do if there are multiple authors of a source?"[13]

Example:

Burawoy, M., Burton, A., Ferguson, A. A., & Fox, K. J. (1991). Ethnography unbound: Power and resistance in the modern metropolis. Berkeley: University of California Press.[14]

Delay, F., Deville, P., Echenoz, J., Greenlee, S., Mathews, H., Polizzotti, M., et al. (1997). S: A novel. Cambridge, MA: Brookline Books.

Book with a Corporate Author:

<Name of corporate author>. (<Publication Year>). <Book Title>. <Place of Publication>: <Publisher>.

Example:

American Psychiatric Association. (1994). Diagnostic and statistical manual of Mental disorders (4th ed.). Washington, DC: Author.[15]

Bertolucci, A. (2005). Winter journey (N. Benson,Trans.). West Lafayette, In: Parlor Press.

Book with an Editor/s:

<Name of editor> .(Ed.). (<Publication Year>). <Title>. <Place of Publication>: <Publisher>.

• If there is more than one editor, write their names the same way as for the authors; abbreviation "Eds." is used for multiple editors

• In the in-text citation, "Ed. or Eds." is not written; instead, the names are mentioned the same way as the authors.[9]

Example:

Johnson, M. H. (Ed.). (1993). Brain development and cognition: A reader. Cambridge, MA: Blackwell.

Book with Multiple Volume:

<Name of author/s>. (<Publication Year>). <Title>. (vol. <mention the volume number>). <Place of Publication>: <Publisher>. Volume number is mentioned in a numeric digit such as 2, 45, 34, etc.[9]

Example:

Trumbach, R. (1998). Sex and gender revolution (Vol. 1). Chicago: University of Chicago Press.

(if more than one volume is used, cite all volumes used)

Pelikan, J. (1975-1991). The Christian tradition: A history of the development of doctrine (Vols. 15). Chicago: University of Chicago Press.

Chapter in an Edited Book:

<Name of chapter's author>. (<Publication Year>). <Chapter title>. In: <name of editor> (Ed.), <Book title> (pp. <range of pages>). <Place of Publication> : <Publisher>.

LeBon, G. (1997). The crowd: A study of the popular mind. In C.D. Ellis (Ed.), The investor's anthology: Original ideas from the industry's greatest minds (pp. 6-12). New York: Wiley.[16]

Electronic Book (e-Book):

<Name/s of author/s>. (<Publication Year>). <Book Title> (<Edition>). <Place of Publication>: <Publisher>. Retrieved from <URL> [17]

• If instead of URL, there is a DOI (digital object identifier), write as follows:

<Name/s of author/s>. (<Publication Year>). <Book Title> (<Edition>). <Place of Publication>: <Publisher>. DOI: <write the DOI address>

Two or more books by the same author published in the same year

Tufte, E. R. (1997a). The visual display of quantitative information (2nd ed.). Cheshire, CT: Graphics Press.

Tufte, E. R. (1997b). Visual explanations: Images and quantities, evidence and narrative. Cheshire, CT: Graphics Press.[18]

iii.   Websites

Page on a Website:

<Name of Author/s>. (<Publication Year>). < page title>. Retrieved <mention the date of retrieval>, from <URL>.

• Date of retrieval refers to the date when you assessed that data from the source

• It is written this way: <MM DD, Y.Y.>; Month (MM) is written in spelling while Day (D.D.) and year (Y.Y.) is written in numeric digits.

Page on a Website Without an Author Name:

<Page title>. (<Publication Year>). Retrieved <mention the date of retrieval>, from <URL>.

• Date of retrieval refers to the date when you assessed that data from the source

• It is written this way: <MM DD, Y.Y.>; Month (MM) is written in spelling while Day (D.D.) and year (Y.Y.) is written in numeric digits.[9]

Facebook Update:

<Name of Author>. (<year, MM DD>). <Title of the post> [Facebook update]. Retrieved from <URL>.

• Day (D.D.) is written as a numeric digit such as 1, 13, 23

• Month (MM) is written in spelling such as January, March etc.

Twitter Update:

<Name of Author>. (<year, MM DD>). <Title of the tweet> [Twitter post]. Retrieved from <URL>.

• If the author's name is used as the Twitter handle, use it as it is without altering it into a sequence of surnames followed by initials.

Blog:

<Name of Author/s>. (<Year, MM DD>). <Page title> [Web blog post]. Retrieved from <URL>.

Example:

Albrecht, K. (2005). Consumers against supermarket privacy invasion and numbering. Retrieved April 22, 2005, from http://www.nocards.org

International Council for Caring Communities. (2005). Retrieved April 22, 2005, from http://www.international-iccc.org

• Degree level refers to the degree for which the thesis has been prepared, such as Ph.D, M.Sc, M.phill etc.[9]

Example:

iv.   Amilhamja,   Published   and   Unpublished Thesis/Dissertation

<Name/s of Author/s>. (<Publication Year>). <title>, (<degree level> thesis), <name of awarding institution> , <place of the institution>

AJ. (2006). Help-Seeking Behaviors and Health Problems of Selected Public Elementary School Teachers in the Division of Sulu, Dissertation, Graduate College, University of Southern Mindanao, Kabacan, Cotabato

v.   Dictionary

Dictionary & Encyclopedia:

<Name of author>. (<Year of publication>). <Title>.<Place of Publication>: <Publisher>

Example:

Gorlusa, M. (2009). Thesaurus for Everyday Use. Makati City Philippines. V3 Printing Corporation

APA Style – Handling Parenthetical Citations

When should you use parenthetical citations?

• When summarizing facts and ideas from a source.

Summarizing means to take ideas from a large passage of another source and condense them using your own words.[20]

• When paraphrasing a source

Paraphrasing means to use the ideas from another source but change the phrasing into your own words.

Keys to using parenthetical citations[21]

For readability:

• Keep references brief

• Give only information needed to identify the source on your reference page

• Do not repeat unnecessary information

Handling quotes in your text

• Author's last name, publication year and page number (s) of quote must appear in the text

e.g. Freud (1996) states that "Juvenile detention is a weak method for correcting delinquency in teenagers", (p. 10).

This style is used when the author's name is used within the quote summary etc.[22]

OR

Juvenile detention is a weak method for correcting delinquency in teenagers (Freud, 2002, p.11)

This style is used when the author's name is not used within the quote, summary etc.

Handling parenthetical citations

Sometimes additional information is necessary when:

• More than one author with the same last name is used.

e.g. (Jean George, 2000; and John George 2002)

• Two or more works are quoted in the same parentheses.

e.g. (George, 1996; Garnett 2002; James, 2004)

• Works with six or more authors.

e.g. (James et. al., 1998)

• Specific part of a source

e.g. (James, 1998, chap. 2)

• If the source has no known author, use an abbreviated version of the title:

e.g. Full Title: "Dancing with the stars" citation in parentheses: ("Dancing," 2005)

• A reference to a personal communication

e.g. Source: E-mail message from John James Citation in parentheses: (John James, personal communication, October 10, 2009)

- A general reference to a website

e.g. Source: University of Guyana website Citation in parentheses: (http://www.uog.edu.gy) [23]

Conjunction and transitional Marker for In-text Citation

a.   In connecting concepts

(likewise, and, more so, moreover, also, in addition, more than, similarly, like, relatively, concurrent to, cognizant to, affirmatively, in juxtaposition, engagingly, connectedly, inter-connectedly, in Correlation, proportionally, congruently)

b.   In citing examples, elaboration, and discussion

(just like, on the same way (hand, end), to enumerate, listed down, somewhat like, for example, to explain, to expound, elaborate, given a chance, to elaborate, substantiate, accordingly, in detail, comprehensively, tantamount to, in capsule, in a nutshell, therefore, in retrospect, clearly, clearly, as per, deemed, subsequently, explicably)

c.   In contrast

(however, on the other hand, on the other end, but, on the other side, compared with, unlike, in contradictory (contrast), paradoxically, opposite wise, on the contrary, reciprocally, oppositely)

d.   In synthesizing

(therefore, thus, hence, henceforth, so that, so, because, that is why, due to, caused by, thereby, in summary, in conclusion, in effect, in turn, definitely, in general, as a whole, holistically, entirely, truly, constantly, logically, operationally, absolutely, apparently)

e.   In transitioning concepts and ideas

(meanwhile, as such, thereby, in a way, consequently, taking side, cognizantly, paramount to, concomitantly, in request for, in favor of, in quest for, looking forward to, behaviorally, emergently)

f.   In stressing a point or position on an issue

(definitely, precisely, absolutely, entirely, irrevocably, soundly, strongly, perfectly, impeccably, intensively, concisely, ultimately, needlessly, seemingly, optimally, preferably,, proportionally, as a ground, as a result, as a matter of fact, in fact, in fact, subsequently, painstakingly, apparently, significantly, incessantly, presumably, legally, competitively, seriously, perfectly, intentionally, essentially, really, immeasurably, enticingly, unquestionably, emphatically, consistently, effectively, efficiently, unconsciously, proportionally, probably, approximately, anticipatedly)

g.   In analyzing idea

(interestingly, vehemently, amazingly, unbelievably, inevitably, intentionally, presumably, notably, remarkably, commandably, impartially, noticeably, sequentially, immeasurably, continuously, untinterruptively, sustainably, seemingly, requisitely, instantly, impressively, accurately, reliably, validly, aggressively, excitingly, dynamically, pertinent to, enthusiastically, tangibly, in accordance to, deemed essential, necessarily, critically)

Guide Word Options for In-text Citation and Data Presentation (for on-text citation)

1. De Leon (2018) stressed that…
2. De Leon (2018) enlisted that…
3. De Leon (2018) asserted that…
4. De Leon (2018) anticipated that…
5. De Leon (2018) defined that…
6. The findings of De Leon (2018) aimed to…
7. The results of De Leon's study (2018) began…
8. The study of De Leon (2018) implied that…
9. According to De Leon (2018) that…
10. The intervention of De Leon (2018) resolved…

11. The idea of De Leon (2018) on research complemented...
12. The study of De Leon (2018) revealed that...
13. The discovery of De Leon (2018) stopped...
14. The study of De Leon (2018) agreed...
15. De Leon (2018) found out that...
16. De Leon (2018) assessed...
17. The study of De Leon (2018) concluded that.. [23]

NOTES

CHAPTER 1: Format and Identifying Research Problems

1. STUDENT THESIS PROPOSAL GUIDELINES.
   http://www.uwindsor.ca/education/sites/uwindsor.ca.e
   ducation/files/student_thesis_proposal_guidelines.pdf
2. Chapter life form any people, most especially - Free ....
   https://lagas.org/chapter-very-useful-in-the-course-of-
   teaching/
3. "Technical Proposal For The Design And Study Of Power
   Supply Network [Tender Documents : T445633976,
   A445633976]." MENA Report, Albawaba (London) Ltd.,
   July 2019.
4. Student and Parent Perspectives on Fipping the
   Mathematics ....
   https://files.eric.ed.gov/fulltext/ED572477.pdf
5. 3 Is there a significant difference in the sustainability ....
   https://www.coursehero.com/file/p7ck4stp/3-Is-there-
   a-significant-difference-in-the-sustainability-of-internet-
   cafe/

CHAPTER 2: Writing the Research Proposal Introduction

1. The Characteristics, Processes, And Ethics Of Research ....
   https://idoc.pub/documents/the-characteristics-
   processes-and-ethics-of-research-wl1pvprkjjlj
2. CHAPTER 5 But.
   https://jacs.weebly.com/uploads/1/2/3/5/1235512/han
   dout_chapter5.pdf
3. Presentation of Chapter 1-3 (Explanation w/ Examples).
   https://www.slideshare.net/AprilCajucom/presentation
   -of-chapter-13-explanation-w-examples
4. PRAC 3 INT.pdf - 1 2 UNIT 1.2 THE NATURE OF
   RESEARCH This ....
   https://www.coursehero.com/file/83059818/PRAC-3-
   INTpdf/
5. NURSING CARE MANAGEMENT 108 – NURSING
   RESEARCH.

http://docshare03.docshare.tips/files/23588/235880670.pdf

6. CHAPTER 5 But.
   https://jacs.weebly.com/uploads/1/2/3/5/1235512/handout_chapter5.pdf
7. Presentation of Chapter 1-3 (Explanation w/ Examples).
   https://www.slideshare.net/AprilCajucom/presentation-of-chapter-13-explanation-w-examples
8. A8561EA3-D62E-48C0-8DDF-170EB6B578DE -
   Organization of ....
   https://www.coursehero.com/file/86043485/A8561EA3-D62E-48C0-8DDF-170EB6B578DE/
9. Factors Associated with Absenteeism in High Schools.
   https://files.eric.ed.gov/fulltext/EJ1097992.pdf
10. Declaration of the Rights of the Child (1959) :: Charter ....
    https://charterforcompassion.org/declaration-of-the-rights-of-the-child-1959
11. Presentation of Chapter 1-3 (Explanation w/ Examples).
    https://www.slideshare.net/AprilCajucom/presentation-of-chapter-13-explanation-w-examples
12. Fighting against "Nothing to hide" - Civil Society's ....
    https://lb.boell.org/en/2018/12/13/fighting-against-nothing-hide-civil-societys-experiences-advocating-data-protection
13. Significance of the Study: 2 Easy Tips on How to Write It.
    https://simplyeducate.me/2015/02/09/significance-of-the-study/
14. University and LUSU join forces to secure future of Green
    ....
    https://scan.lancastersu.co.uk/2015/04/30/university-and-lusu-join-forces-to-secure-future-of-green-lancaster/
15. Interpersonal relations: The key to effective school ....
    https://scholarworks.lib.csusb.edu/cgi/viewcontent.cgi?referer=&httpsredir=1&article=1343&context=etd-project
16. CHAPTER I INTRODUCTION 1.1 Background of the
    Study.
    http://repository.unair.ac.id/96393/4/4.%20CHAPTER%20I%20-%20INTRODUCTION.pdf

Chapter 3: Writing the Research Proposal Review of Related Literature

1. Collective or Farmer: Land Ownership in North Korea - Daily NK. https://www.dailynk.com/english/collective-or-farmer-land-ownershi/

2. The strengths and limitations of the research methodology. http://www.expertsmind.com/library/the-strengths-and-limitations-of-the-research-methodology-5516381.aspx

3. Interpersonal relations: The key to effective school .... https://scholarworks.lib.csusb.edu/cgi/viewcontent.cgi?referer=&httpsredir=1&article=1343&context=etd-project

4. Effective Supervision. https://www3.nd.edu/~jthomp19/AS300/2_Spring%20Semester/Effective_Supervision_V2.pdf

Chapter 4: Writing the Research Proposal Methodology

1. STUDENT THESIS PROPOSAL GUIDELINES. http://www.uwindsor.ca/education/sites/uwindsor.ca.education/files/student_thesis_proposal_guidelines.pdf

2. All Stuffs in One: Guidelines to write Thesis Proposal for MBA. https://everystuffsinone.blogspot.com/2019/02/guidelines-to-write-thesis-proposal-for.html

3. STUDENT THESIS PROPOSAL GUIDELINES. http://web4.uwindsor.ca/units/edu/masters/main.nsf/cf50c73c23e058b985256db30060a59e/d7710f12b3f1da69852574ab00676d80/$FILE/STUDENT%20THESIS%20PROPOSAL%20GUIDELINES.pdf

4. CHAPTER III RESEARCH METHODOLOGY. http://a-research.upi.edu/operator/upload/s_c5051_056168_chapter3.pdf

5. It also ascertains how much variation is caused by another
   .... https://www.coursehero.com/file/p4cjeif/It-also-
   ascertains-how-much-variation-is-caused-by-another-
   variable-Measure-to/

6. DOCUMENT RESUME HE 002 942 AUTHOR DuVall
   Charles R.; And ....
   https://files.eric.ed.gov/fulltext/ED061882.pdf

7. Research procedure | Eddusaver.
   https://www.eddusaver.com/research-procedure/

CHAPTER 5: Citing Sources

1. Citation help - University of Victoria.
   https://www.uvic.ca/library/help/citation/index.php

2. Citation Help - Political Science - LibGuides at ....
   https://libguides.uvic.ca/polisci/citation

3. Usage of Computers and internet for teaching and
   learning ....
   https://ir.ucc.edu.gh/xmlui/handle/123456789/2612

4. Rewards - Rita's Ice. https://www.ritasice.com/rewards/

5. Lesson 15 following ethical standards in writing literature.
   https://www.slideshare.net/mjlobetos/lesson-15-
   following-ethical-standards-in-writing-literature

6. Quoting and Paraphrasing – The Writing Center – UW–
   Madison.
   https://writing.wisc.edu/handbook/assignments/quotin
   gsources/

7. Lesson 15 following ethical standards in writing literature.
   https://www.slideshare.net/mjlobetos/lesson-15-
   following-ethical-standards-in-writing-literature

8. GUIDELINES FOR THE RESPONSIBLE CONDUCT OF
   RESEARCH.
   https://www.provost.pitt.edu/sites/default/files/GUID

ELINES%20FOR%20ETHICAL%20PRACTICES%20IN%2
0RESEARCH-V.2%20FINAL%207-15-16.pdf

9. (PDF) A Manual for Referencing Styles in Research.
https://www.researchgate.net/publication/308786787_A
_Manual_for_Referencing_Styles_in_Research

10. MEMORIES OF AN EMOTIONAL AND A
NONEMOTIONAL EVENT: EFFECTS ....
https://sites.oxy.edu/clint/physio/article/memoriesofan
emotionalandanonemotionalevent.pdf

11. Interpersonal Accuracy and Interaction Outcomes: Why
and ....
https://link.springer.com/chapter/10.1007%2F978-3-030-
34964-6_11

12. Differences in emotional intelligence between effective ....
https://journals.sagepub.com/doi/abs/10.1177/0020852
311399857

13. (PDF) A Manual for Referencing Styles in Research.
https://www.researchgate.net/publication/308786787_A
_Manual_for_Referencing_Styles_in_Research

14. Burawoy, Michael. "Forty Years Of Labor 12." Michigan
Sociological Review, vol. 29, Michigan Sociological
Association, Oct. 2015, p. 1.

15. Fornari, Victor. "Review of Care of Children Exposed to
the Traumatic Effects of Disaster, by Jon A. Shaw, Zelde
Espinel, and James M. Shultz." Journal of Child and
Adolescent Psychopharmacology, vol. 24, no. 9, Mary Ann
Liebert, Inc., Nov. 2014, p. 532.

16. Copley, Gregory. "The Global Tectonic Plates Begin to
Move." Defense & Foreign Affairs Strategic Policy, vol. 43,
no. 8, International Strategic Studies Association, Aug.
2015, p. 4.

17. Two or More Books by the Same Author | Open
Textbooks for ....
https://www.opentextbooks.org.hk/ditatopic/4966

18. Takahashi, Tess. "Data Visualization as Documentary Form: The Murmur of Digital Magnitude." Discourse, vol. 39, no. 3, Wayne State University Press, Oct. 2017, p. 376.

19. English for Academic Purposes (EAP). http://wwwdata.unibg.it/dati/corsi/640005/78361-EAP3.pdf

20. APA (3-28-17) - Documenting Sources Using APA Format https://www.coursehero.com/file/23639736/APA-3-28-17/

21. Cross referencing using MLA style. https://www.slideshare.net/khuramdad/cross-referencing-using-mla-style

22. APA - Help Citing Sources - Guides at Central Oregon .... https://guides.cocc.edu/citations/apa

23. In-Text Citations - ASA Style - Research Guides at .... https://guides.library.unk.edu/c.php?g=510530&p=3488886